BOOKS BY JAMES WRIGHT

The Green Wall
Saint Judas
The Branch Will Not Break
Shall We Gather at the River
Collected Poems
Two Citizens
Moments of the Italian Summer
To a Blossoming Pear Tree
This Journey

THIS JOURNEY

THIS JOURNEY

JAMES WRIGHT

RANDOM HOUSE
NEW YORK

"The Turtle Overnight," "Dawn Near an Old Battlefield, in a Time
of Peace," "At the End of Sirmione," "Jerome in Solitude," "A
Mouse Taking a Nap," "Taranto," "Time," "In Memory of
the Ottomans," and "Regret for a Spider Web" were
first published in *Antaeus*.

"Coming Home to Maui," "The Ice House," and "The Sumac in
Ohio" were first published in *The Ohio Review*.

"Sheep in the Rain," "A Flower Passage," "Your Name in Arezzo,"
"Venice," "Between Wars," "Against Surrealism," and "May
Morning" were first published in *Poetry*.

"This and That" and "In View of the Protestant Cemetery in
Rome" by James Wright first appeared in the *Nation*, 1981.
Copyright © 1981 Nation Magazine, The Nation Associates, Inc.
Reprinted by permission.

Other selections appeared in the following publications: *American
Poetry Review, Choice, Clifton, Country Journal, Crazy Horse, Durak,
Georgia Review, Harper's, Harvard, Hudson Review, Ironwood, Montana
Review, The Nation, The New Yorker, Paris Review, Three Rivers
Poetry Review.*

Library of Congress Cataloging in Publication Data

Wright, James Arlington, 1927–1980
This journey.

I. Title.
PS3545.R58T5   811'.54   81-15691
ISBN 0-394-52365-2   AACR2

Manufactured in the United States of America

2 4 6 8 9 7 5 3

FIRST EDITION

To the city of Fano
Where we got well
From Annie and me

ACKNOWLEDGMENTS

In gratitude to the John Simon Guggenheim Memorial Foundation for the generous grant that helped James Wright finish this book.

With abiding love to Robert Bly, Hayden Carruth, Donald Hall, Galway Kinnell, John Logan, Robert Mezey and Helen Wright for their help in the preparation of *This Journey*.

CONTENTS

THIS JOURNEY

ENTERING THE TEMPLE IN NÎMES

As long as this evening lasts,
I am going to walk all through and around
The Temple of Diana.
I hope to pay my reverence to the goddess there
Whom the young Romans loved.
Though they learned her name from the dark rock
Among bearded Greeks,
It was here in the south of Gaul they found her true
To her own solitude.
For here surely the young women of Gaul
Glanced back thoughtfully over their bare
White shoulders and hurried away
Out of sight and then rose, reappearing
As vines and the pale inner hands of sycamores
In the green places.
This evening, in winter,
I pray for the stone-eyed legions of the rain
To put off their armor.
Allow me to walk between the tall pillars
And find the beginning of one vine leaf there,
Though I arrive too late for the last spring
And the rain still mounts its guard.

THIS AND THAT

I am not going to share
Those high, those delicate
Cheekbones with her.
Nor the light feet I saw
Walking beneath the long
Stems, lovely of youth.

I am not going to name
The place where usual men
Pronounced on her
A heavy ritual stone.
They were all right, those men.
They didn't know.

In a panic once, she blurted
She loved me, and I had
Too much to say.
If I had only shared
The silences, she would
Have been all right.

But, no, I had to intone
A long harangue about
The this, the that.
Now this and that are gone,
And the high delicate
Bones are gone.

Light feet I saw walking
Bewildered by long stems,
She walked away.
And still I sit here talking.
And I still have, it seems,
The east wind to say.

COME, LOOK QUIETLY

The bird on the terrace has his own name in French, but I don't know it. He may be a nuthatch, only he doesn't eat upside down.

He has a perfectly round small purple cap on his crown and a slender long mask from his ears to his eyes all the way across. Come, look quietly. All the way across Paris. Far behind the bird, the globes of Sacré Coeur form out of the rain and fade again, all by themselves. The daylight all across the city is taking its own time.

The plump Parisian wild bird is scoring a light breakfast at the end of December. He has found the last seeds left in tiny cones on the outcast Christmas tree that blows on the terrace.

OLD BUD

Old Bud Romick weighed three hundred pounds if he weighed an ounce, and he weighed an ounce. He used to sit on his front porch swing, enraged and helpless, while his two tiny grandchildren, hilarious and hellish little boys, scampered just out of his reach and yelled hideously, "Hell on you, Grandpa." His unbelievable Adam's apple purpled and shone like the burl on the root of a white oak, and he sang his God Damns in despair.

Old Bud Romick has fallen asleep as the twilight comes down Pearl Street in Martins Ferry, Ohio. The window shutters close here and there, and the flowing streetcars glow past into silence, their wicker seats empty, for the factory whistles have all blown down, and the widows all gone home. Empty, too, are the cinder alleys, smelling of warm summer asphalt. The streetlight columns, faintly golden, fill with the cracked mirrors of June bugs' wings. Old Bud Romick sags still on the porch swing. The rusty chains do their best for his body in the dark.

The dark turns around him, a stain like the bruise on a plum somebody somehow missed and left under a leaf. His two hellions have long since giggled their way upstairs. Old Bud Romick is talking lightly in his sleep, and an evening shower brings him a sticky new sycamore leaf in his sleep.

Whether or not he is aware of leaves, I don't know. I don't know whether or not he is aware of anything touching his face. Whether or not he dreams of how slender sycamores are, how slender young women are when they walk beneath the trees without caring how green they are, how lucky a plum might be if it dies without being eaten, I don't know.

THE TURTLE OVERNIGHT

I remember him last twilight in his comeliness. When it began to rain, he appeared in his accustomed place and emerged from his accustomed place and emerged from his shell as far as he could reach—feet, legs, tail, head. He seemed to enjoy the rain, the sweet-tasting rain that blew all the way across lake water to him from the mountains, the Alto Adige. It was as near as I've ever come to seeing a turtle take a pleasant bath in his natural altogether. All the legendary faces of broken old age disappeared from my mind, the thickened muscles under the chins, the nostrils brutal with hatred, the murdering eyes. He filled my mind with a sweet-tasting mountain rain, his youthfulness, his modesty as he washed himself all alone, his religious face.

For a long time now this morning, I have been sitting at this window and watching the grass below me. A moment ago there was no one there. But now his brindle shell sighs slowly up and down in the midst of the green sunlight. A black watchdog snuffles asleep just beyond him, but I trust that neither is afraid of the other. I can see him lifting his face. It is a raising of eyebrows toward the light, an almost imperceptible turning of the chin, an ancient pleasure, an eagerness.

Along his throat there are small folds, dark yellow as pollen shaken across a field of camomila. The lines on his face suggest only a relaxation, a delicacy in the understanding of the grass, like the careful tenderness I saw once on the face of a hobo in Ohio as he waved greeting to an empty wheat field from the flatcar of a freight train.

But now the train is gone, and the turtle has left his circle of empty grass. I look a long time where he was, and I can't find a footprint in the empty grass. So much air left, so much sunlight, and still he is gone.

THE SUMAC IN OHIO

Toward the end of May, the air in southern Ohio is filling with fragrances, and I am a long way from home. A great place lies open in the earth there in Martins Ferry near the river, and to this day I don't know how it came to be. Maybe the old fathers of my town, their white hair lost long since into the coal smoke and the snow, gathered in their hundreds along the hither side of the B&O railroad track, presented whatever blades and bull tongues they could spare, and tore the earth open. Or maybe the gulley appeared there on its own, long before the white-haired fathers came, and the Ohio changed its direction, and the glacier went away.

But now toward the end of May, the sumac trees on the slopes of the gulley are opening their brindle buds, and suddenly, right before my eyes, the tough leaf branches turn a bewildering scarlet just at the place where they join the bough. You can strip the long leaves away already, but the leaf branch is more thoroughly rooted into the tree than the trunk itself is into the ground.

Before June begins, the sap and coal smoke and soot from Wheeling steel, wafted down the Ohio by some curious gentleness in the Appalachians, will gather all over the trunk. The skin will turn aside hatchets and knife blades. You cannot even carve a girl's name on the sumac. It is viciously determined to live and die alone, and you can go straight to hell.

READING A 1979 INSCRIPTION ON BELLI'S MONUMENT

It is not only the Romans who are gone.
Belli, unhappy a century ago,
Won from the world his fashionable stone.
Where it stands now, he doesn't even know.
Across the Tiber, near Trastevere,
His top hat teetered on his head with care,
Brushed like a gentleman, he cannot see
The latest Romans who succeed him there.

One of them bravely climbed his pedestal
And sprayed a scarlet MERDA on his shawl.
This afternoon, I pray his hidden grave
Lies nameless somewhere in the hills, while rain
Fusses and frets to rinse away the stain.
Rain might erase when marble cannot save.

CONTEMPLATING THE FRONT STEPS
OF THE CATHEDRAL IN FLORENCE
AS THE CENTURY DIES

Once, in some hill trees long ago,
A red-tailed hawk paused
Long enough to look me over
Halfway down the air.
He held still, and plainly
Said, go.
It was no time
For singing about the beauties of nature,
And I went fast.
I stubbed my toe
On a rock hidden by the big wing-shadows,
But the small wound
Was worth paying for.
I got one glimpse of him,
Alive, before I die.
And that is all I know
About his body.

It would be easy
To touch the snaggle of infected meat
In front of me now.
But the blowflies
Have got to it first.
The maggots have burrowed
Up one collapsing thigh.
The body, even in death,
Flinches and hides one wing
Behind it, but already
A mass of slick green beetles
Have crawled around there.

I do not want to join them, I want
To leave the last wing
Alone to the beetles and the maggots.
Let them have Giotto's long wing stretched out in the terrible sunlight.
Maybe they will rend one another
And explode.

WHEREVER HOME IS

Leonardo da Vinci, haggard in basalt stone,
Will soon be gone,
A frivolous face lost in wisteria flowers.
They are turning gray and dying
All over his body.
Subtlest of all wanderers
Who live beautifully by living on other lives,
They cannot find a warm vein
In Leonardo, and Leonardo
Himself will soon
Be gone.

Good riddance a little while to the insane.
Although the wisteria gets nowhere
And the sea wind crumbles Leonardo down,
A new lizard frolics in the cold sunlight
Between Leonardo's thumb and his palette.
One brief lizard
Lavishes on Leonardo and on me
The whole spring.

Goodbye to Leonardo, good riddance
To decaying madmen who cannot keep alive
The wanderers among trees.
I am going home with the lizard,
Wherever home is,
And lie beside him unguarded
In the clear sunlight.
We will lift our faces even if it rains.
We will both turn green.

A DARK MOOR BIRD

A dark moor bird has come down from the mountains
To test the season.
He flies low across the Adige and seines
The brilliant web of his shadow behind him.
Slender and sure,
His wings give him the nobility
Of a small swan.
But his voice
Ruins it, he has seen me and he can't
Shut up about it.
He sounds
Like a plump chicken nagging a raccoon
Who is trying to get out of the henhouse
With a little dignity.

I wonder why the beautiful moor bird
Won't leave me alone.
All I am doing is standing here,
Turning to stone,
Believing he will build a strong nest
Along the Adige, hoping
He will never die.

NOTES OF A PASTORALIST

In a field outside of Pisa, I saw a shepherd
Keeping warm from a late autumn day.
Blown a little
To one side by the cooling sunlight,
He leaned as though a good tree were holding
His body upright.
But the nearest cypresses
Were standing a long way off,
And it seemed that only his green umbrella
Held him there.
His sheep did not flock together
As they do in Spenser and Theocritus.
They ambled all over the slope
Too old to care
Or too young to know they were posing
For the notes
Of a jaded pastoralist.
If the shepherd had a tune,
I stood too far away to hear it.
I hope he sang to himself. I didn't feel
Like paying him to sing.

THE VESTAL IN THE FORUM

This morning I do not despair
For the impersonal hatred that the cold
Wind seems to feel
When it slips fingers into the flaws
Of lovely things men made,
The shoulders of a stone girl
Pitted by winter.
Not a spring passes but the roses
Grow stronger in their support of the wind,
And now they are conquerors,
Not garlands any more,
Of this one face:
Dimming,
Clearer to me than most living faces.
The slow wind and the slow roses
Are ruining an eyebrow here, a mole there.
But in this little while
Before she is gone, her very haggardness
Amazes me. A dissolving
Stone, she seems to change from stone to something
Frail, to someone I can know, someone
I can almost name.

IN VIEW OF THE
PROTESTANT CEMETERY IN ROME

It is idle to say
The wind will blow your fingers all away
And scatter small blue knucklebones upon
The ground from hell to breakfast and beyond.
You will sit listening till I am gone
To seed among the pear trees. For my voice
Sprinkles a few light petals on this pond,
And you nod sagely, saying I am wise.
Your fingers toss their white cocoons and rise
Lightly and lightly brush against my face:
Alive still, in this violated place,
Idle as any deed that Cestius did,
Vanished beneath his perfect pyramid.

ABOVE SAN FERMO

Somehow I have never lost
That feeling of astonished flight,
When the breath of my body suddenly
Becomes visible.

I might be standing beside a black snowdrift
in Ohio, where the railroad gravel
And the mill smoke that gets everything in the end
Reveal the true colors
Of a bewildered winter.
When I lit a match and breathed there,
A solitary batwing sailed out of my mouth
And hovered, fluttering,
All the way over to West Virginia
And beyond.

Even now,
Abandoned beside the abandoned battlements
Above the Adige, above
San Fermo, a hand waves over my lungs.
The demon leaps out
And takes off his hand-me-down jacket.
He strolls downhill
In the warm Italian sunlight, as though
He didn't care to choose between winter and spring.
But spring will do him all right,
For the time being.

A REPLY TO MATTHEW ARNOLD ON
MY FIFTH DAY IN FANO

("In harmony with Nature? Restless
fool . . . Nature and man can never be
fast friends. . . .")

It is idle to speak of five mere days in Fano, or five long days, or five years. As I prepare to leave, I seem to have just arrived. To carefully split yet another infinitive, I seem to have been here forever or longer, longer than the sea's lifetime and the lifetimes of all the creatures of the sea, than all the new churches among the hill pastures and all the old shells wandering about bodiless just off the clear shore. Briefly in harmony with nature before I die, I welcome the old curse:

a restless fool and a fast friend to Fano, I have brought this wild chive flower down from a hill pasture. I offer it to the Adriatic. I am not about to claim that the sea does not care. It has its own way of receiving seeds, and today the sea may as well have a flowering one, with a poppy to float above it, and the Venetian navy underneath. Goodbye to the living place, and all I ask it to do is stay alive.

PETITION TO THE TERNS

I have lived long enough to see
Many wings fall
And many others broken and driven
To stagger away on a slant
Of wind. It blows
Where it pleases to blow,
Or it poises,
Unaccountably,
At rest. Today, sails
Don't move.
In the water,
In front of my eyes,
The huge dull scarlet men-of-war loll, uncaring and slobbish,
And stain
All the shore shallows
That men might hope to become
Green among.
The sea
Is already unfriendly.
The terns of Rhode Island
Dart up out of the cattails, pounce on the sunlight,
Claim it,
And attack.
They must be getting their own back,
Against the wind. But the wind is no angrier
Than any wing it blows down,
And I wish the terns would give it
And me a break.

IN GALLIPOLI

Gray as the sea moss wavering among the green shallows along the shore, her hair blows shaggy. The sky holds. She lifts a cluster of grapes, aloof and strangely sacred in their frost, and urges them on me. Forty years ago, her young man, as gray and unaware as an English butterfly blinded by fog, fluttered amazed across this cerulean light, sagged, and exploded. I select two or three purple grapes, and one of them bursts inside my mouth. But they are not nearly enough for her to give, and she urges me on and on, till all she holds in her fingers is the hulled branch of the vine. It sways like a tree set on fire and thrown into water. She looks into the sky. It holds. All her offerings are gone.

THE LIMPET IN OTRANTO

These limpets have lain empty and bodiless for long years now. Flecks of brown gold gather on their slopes like old flowers on hills at the end of autumn. They shine, even when the sun has gone down. Virgil approached them and listened inside them. But their caves were too shallow and bright to contain any ghosts. Their bodies were already gone a long time into the air. Cloud shadows and the shadows of scarred headlands fell all over the old man's shoulders, like oak leaves, the old everlasting bronzes of November, the tragic sea-faces of the trees in North Carolina, that tremble and grow older all through the year, but never fall. Caressing the inner side of a limpet with one finger, Virgil turned back inland. The purple of thistles aristocratically brushed his knees aside. He heard a voice in a tree, crying in Greek, "Italy. Italy." He listened again to the limpet in his hand. It said nothing.

APOLLO

A young man, his face dark
With the sea's fire,
Quickens his needle bone through webbing,
and passes away.
He moves out of my sight
And back again, as the moon
Braces its shoulders and disappears
And appears again. The young face
Begins to turn gray
In the evening light that cannot
Make up for loss.
It is morning and evening again, all over the water.
I know it is only moonlight that changes him, I know
It does not matter. The sea's fire
Is only the cold shadow of the moon's,
And the moon's
Fire itself only the cold
Shadow of the young
Fisherman's face:
The only home where now, alone in the evening,
The god stays alive.

MAY MORNING

Deep into spring, winter is hanging on. Bitter and skillful in his hopeless-ness, he stays alive in every shady place, starving along the Mediterranean: angry to see the glittering sea-pale boulder alive with lizards green as Judas leaves. Winter is hanging on. He still believes. He tries to catch a lizard by the shoulder. One olive tree below Grottaglie welcomes the winter into noontime shade, and talks as softly as Pythagoras. Be still, be patient, I can hear him say, cradling in his arms the wounded head, letting the sunlight touch the savage face.

A TRUE VOICE
(for Robert Bly)

In northern Minnesota the floors of the earth are covered with white sand. Even after the sun has gone down beyond the pine trees and the moon has not yet come across the lake water, you can walk down white roads. The dark is a dark you can see beyond, into a deep place here and there. Whatever light there is left, it has room enough to move around in. The tall thick pines have all disappeared after the sun. That is why the small blue spruces look so friendly when your eyes feel at home in the dark. I never touched a blue spruce before the moon came, for fear it would say something in a false voice. You can only hear a spruce tree speak in its own silence.

CHILBLAIN

My uncle Willy with his long lecherous face
Once told me wisely:
Over in France in them cathouses
In the big war,
They used to sell a salve,
That you squeezed on the inside
Of your forefinger knuckle,
And it spread all over.
Sure, it didn't cure chilblain.
But it stung so bad it took
Your mind off your troubles.

He snickered darkly, without sound,
The proud man's wisdom.

Willy the liar is buried in Colrain,
And every time in dreams I see him there
The violets and snowflakes run
Together, till all June
Earth smokes like slag.
Violets and snowflakes gather, gather
In a mock caress,
And Willy's stone clenches shut like a young man's hand
Frightened of France and winter.
Before I wake, the stone remembers
Where it is, where Ohio is,
Where violets last only a little.
Mill-smoke kills them halfway through spring,
And chilblain still stings
In June when earth smokes like slag.

COMING HOME TO MAUI

It took her an hour to climb the green cliff here.
She rose as the light rose. Now,
On this small pinnacle, the long-legged brown girl,
American from Chicago, places
One glittering opihi shell,
Bony with light,
Into my pale hand.

One afternoon in the dark howling
Of ice off Lake Michigan,
She blundered into a bewildered young man,
A Hawaiian lost on State Street.
So she brought him home.

Now, as we stand here, the young man searches
Below us, down, into the ocean.
He is hunting for shellfish
Among the strange trees.
He brings the opihi home in the evening,
And she shines them.

He makes a living
Grounging under water before sunrise and after.
He turns home toward the woman,
He turns the dark creatures of his ocean
Over to the woman,
And soon they shine.

Years ago, far from home, I came to these islands.
I had rolled, puking in a dark shell,
A troopship, all of two nights.

Then, when I woke,
It was hard to believe the earth
Could be lived on at all, much less the beautiful

Home of this woman's hands, home of this light.
And yet here it is, this green cliff where she rose,
The home of this light.

AGAINST SURREALISM

There are some tiny obvious details in human life that survive the divine purpose of boring fools to death. In France, all the way down south in Avallon, people like to eat cake. The local bakers there spin up a little flour and chocolate into the shape of a penguin. We came back again and again to a certain window to admire a flock of them. But we never bought one.

We found ourselves wandering through Italy, homesick for penguins.

Then a terrible and savage fire of the dog-days roared all over the fourteenth arondissement: which is to say, it was August: and three chocolate penguins appeared behind a window near Place Denfert-Rochereau. We were afraid the Parisians would recognize them, so we bought them all and snuck them home under cover.

We set them out on a small table above half the rooftops of Paris. I reached out to brush a tiny obvious particle of dust from the tip of a beak. Suddenly the dust dropped an inch and hovered there. Then it rose to the beak again.

It was a blue spider.

If I were a blue spider, I would certainly ride on a train all the way from Avallon to Paris, and I would set up my house on the nose of a chocolate penguin. It's just a matter of common sense.

THE ICE HOUSE

The house was really a cellar deep beneath the tower of the old Belmont Brewery. My father's big shoulders heaved open the door from the outside, and from within the big shoulders of the ice-man leaned and helped. The slow door gave. My brother and I walked in delighted by our fear, and laid our open palms on the wet yellow sawdust. Outside the sun blistered the paint on the corrugated roofs of the shacks by the railroad; but we stood and breathed the rising steam of that amazing winter, and carried away in our wagon the immense fifty-pound diamond, while the old man chipped us each a jagged little chunk and then walked behind us, his hands so calm they were trembling for us, trembling with exquisite care.

THE JOURNEY

Anghiari is medieval, a sleeve sloping down
A steep hill, suddenly sweeping out
To the edge of a cliff, and dwindling.
But far up the mountain, behind the town,
We too were swept out, out by the wind,
Alone with the Tuscan grass.

Wind had been blowing across the hills
For days, and everything now was graying gold
With dust, everything we saw, even
Some small children scampering along a road,
Twittering Italian to a small caged bird.
We sat beside them to rest in some brushwood,
And I leaned down to rinse the dust from my face.

I found the spider web there, whose hinges
Reeled heavily and crazily with the dust,
Whole mounds and cemeteries of it, sagging
And scattering shadows among shells and wings.
And then she stepped into the center of air
Slender and fastidious, the golden hair
Of daylight along her shoulders, she poised there,
While ruins crumbled on every side of her.
Free of the dust, as though a moment before
She had stepped inside the earth, to bathe herself.

I gazed, close to her, till at last she stepped
Away in her own good time.

Many men
Have searched all over Tuscany and never found
What I found there, the heart of the light
Itself shelled and leaved, balancing
On filaments themselves falling. The secret

Of this journey is to let the wind
Blow its dust all over your body,
To let it go on blowing, to step lightly, lightly
All the way through your ruins, and not to lose
Any sleep over the dead, who surely
Will bury their own, don't worry.

YOUNG WOMEN AT CHARTRES

(in memory of Jean Garrigue)

> ". . . like a thief I followed her
> Though my heart was so alive
> I thought it equal to that beauty."
> ("THE STRANGER")

ONE

Halfway through morning
Lisa, herself blossoming, strolls
Lazily beneath the eastern roses
In the shadow of Chartres.
She does not know
She is visible.
As she lifts her face
Toward the northwest,
Mothwings fall down and rest on her hair.
She darkens
Without knowing it, as the wind blows on down toward the river
Where the cathedral, last night,
Sank among reeds.

TWO

Fog
Rinses away for a little while the cold
Christs with their suffering faces.
Mist
Leaves to us solitary friends of the rain
The happy secret angel
On the north corner.

THREE

You lived so abounding with mist and wild strawberries,
So faithful with the angel in the rain,
You kept faith to a stranger.
Now, Jean, your musical name poises in the webs
Of wheatfield and mist,
And beneath the molded shadow of the local stones,

I hear you again, singing beneath the northwest
Angel who holds in her arms
Sunlight on sunlight.
She is equal
To you, to her own happy face, she is holding
A sundial in her arms. No wonder Christ was happy
Among women's faces.

TO THE CICADA

(Anacreon)

A few minutes ago
I got up out of the burlap rags somebody
Flung last night into the corner
Of the stone floor.

I am standing here in the field.
I have got my back turned on the whitewashed wall of the house.
The sunlight glances off it and flays
The back of my neck.

It's not yet noon,
But noon is gathering and solidifying,
Splotching my shoulders.
My eyelids weigh ten pounds. Nevertheless,
I lift them open with my fingers.
It's hard to bend the joints.

But there it is,
On the other side of the field,
The water barrel, the only real thing
Left in the shadow.
I can see the rust-stained bung dribbling
Its cold slaver down the curved slats,
Squiggling into black muck beneath
The barbed-wire fence.

Here, now,
Sick of the dry dirt, the southern barrenness,
The Ohio hillside twenty-five miles lost
Away from the river,
I feel my shoulders grow heavier and heavier,
And the dead corn-blades coiling,
Stinging my thighs.
Here,
Just as in the airless corner

Of the barn over the hill
The disinfected hooks stand arranged
Along one wall at head height,
Where the farmer has screwed them in;
Just there where he'd hung them after he'd finished
Dusting out the doorway, hopelessly scattering
Stray wheat beards, tiny dry blossoms of hay,
Mouse droppings, cow pies jagged and cruel
As old gravestones knocked down and scarred faceless;
And just as the meat hooks, gleaming softly, hold
Long sidemeat crusted with salt and the dull hams
Gone rigid with smoke,
And the hooks creak as the meat sags, just so
My bones sag and hold up
The flesh of my body.

Still, now, I hear you, singing,
A lightness beginning among the dark crevices,
In the underbark of the locust, beyond me,
The other edge of the field.
A lightness,
You begin tuning up for your time,
Twilight, that belongs to you, deeper and cooler beyond
The barbed wire of this field, even beyond
The Ohio River twenty-five miles away,
Where the Holy Rollers rage all afternoon
And all evening among the mud cracks,
The polluted shore, their voices splintering
Like beetles' wings in a hobo jungle fire,
Their voices heavy as blast furnace fumes, their brutal
Jesus risen but dumb.

But you, lightness,
Light flesh singing lightly,
Trembling in perfect balance on the underbark,

The locust tree of the southeast, you, friendly
To whatever sings in me as it climbs and holds on
Among the damp brambles:

You, lightness,
How were you born in this place, this heavy stone
Plummeting into the stars?
And still you are here. One morning
I found you asleep on a locust root, and carefully
I breathed on your silver body speckled with brown
And held you a while in my palm
And let you sleep.
You, lightness, kindlier than my human body,
Yet somehow friendly to the music in my body,
I let you sleep, one of the gods who will rise
Without being screamed at.

LIGHTNING BUGS ASLEEP
IN THE AFTERNOON

These long-suffering and affectionate shadows,
These fluttering jewels, are trying to get
Some sleep in a dry shade beneath the cement
Joists of the railroad trestle.

I did not climb up here to find them.
It was only my ordinary solitude
I was following up here this afternoon.
Last evening I sat here with a girl.

It was a dangerous place to be a girl
And young. But she simply folded her silent
Skirt over bare knees, printed with the flowered cotton
Of a meal sack her mother had stitched for her.

Neither of us said anything to speak of.
These affectionate, these fluttering bodies
Signaled to one another under the bridge
While the B&O 40-and-8's rattled away.

Now ordinary and alone in the afternoon,
I find this little circle of insects
Common as soot, clustering on dim stone,
Together with their warm secrets.

I think I am going to leave them folded
And sleeping in their slight gray wings.
I think I am going to climb back down
And open my eyes and shine.

GREETINGS IN NEW YORK CITY

A man walking alone, a stranger
In a strange forest,
Plucks his way carefully among brambles.
He ploughs the spider pits.
He is awake and lonely in the midday,
The jungle of the sun.

He steps out of the snaggle, naked.

A hundred yards away,
One more stranger steps out of the dank vines,
Into the clearing.

Nothing is alone any more.

Two alone, two hours, they poise there,
Afraid, gazing across.

Then,
The green masses behind one shoulder
Cluster their grapes together,
And they become night. And by night each stranger
Turns back into a tree and lies down,
A root, alone.

Sleepless by dawn,
One rises
And finds the other already awake,
Gazing.
Weary,
He lifts his hand and shades his eyes.

Startled,
He touches his chin.

The other stranger across the distance
Touches his chin.
He pauses, then leans down,
And lifts a stone.
The other stranger leans down
And lifts a stone.

All the long morning
They edge the clearing
With little patterns of stones.
Sometimes they balance
Three pebbles on boulders
Or patterns of stars.
Or they lay out new flowers
In circles
Or little gatherings of faces
That neither stranger
Had ever seen.

And then, when noon comes,
Each stranger
Has no room left in the light
Except for only his hands.
Here are mine. They are kind of skinny. May I have your lovely trees?

TO THE SILVER SWORD
SHINING ON THE EDGE
OF THE CRATER

Strange leaves on Haleakala,
My torn home,
You have no family among orchids, African tulips.
Or plumeria and their children.

Yet you lift your face
Ten thousand feet above trees here, and trees here
Are also strange presences among the rest.
We rend one another.

Opening on one of the highest pinnacles
Of light we have left,
You look like a lonesomeness
From somewhere else.

I am not a stranger here.
I stand beside you and gaze over ninety miles of water.
Not long ago, many young men golden in the light of the human body
Killed one another so horribly

They bloated the azure ocean
Into a brilliant scarlet shadow.
O lovely stranger, sometimes in this place we do not even allow
The night to heal us.

Whoever you are,
Who may have made some kind gesture
To me on my earth, you are welcome
To me and mine.

Look, I bring you a wild thing,
A token of welcome, a withered thing,

A human hand. Sometimes the strange creatures
Ten thousand feet below us who somehow

Go on living near waters
Give these things to each other.
And sometimes things like these go searching
Along dark paths, and find trees there,

And blossoms in tall rain.

WITH THE GIFT OF AN
ALABASTER TORTOISE

One afternoon, we stole
Away, we two, around
The whole wall of Arezzo,
A town of golden shadow.
Behind one wall, we found
One lizard, who was whole.

You led me to that place
Where I had never gone.
No, where I'd had no song
Nor prayer of anything.
You stood, still on the stone.
You touched my face.

I gazed at the green shoulder
And the golden long tail,
Magnificent, and quick.
I stood low in the thick
Pines of Arezzo, still
As Dante, and no older.

What the air sang me then
Was simple, and enough:
No, I would never find
How far God's terrible wind
Could whirl me out of love,
Across, or up, or down.

That lizard, green and gone,
Still lives his life among
Those crevices ago.
Would I have caught him? No.
I listened to the song
You sang, still on the stone.

I let time pass, and went
Alone up a long hill,
Volterra, the tawny city
Trembling above Tuscany,
Where the air hovered still
Like a dumb lament.

Behind your back, I found
A stone some girl had molded
And polished into this
Small alabaster tortoise;
I carried it, and folded
Your voice, and made no sound.

The living lizard stays
Far off in Arezzo,
While now this little stone
Waits for your hand alone
To warm its Casentino
And lift its face.

You will raise it above
That Casentino where
The air sings beyond song.
It will shine among
Your glittering hands in the air
And then it will move.

SMALL WILD CRABS DELIGHTING ON BLACK SAND

Nearsighted, I feel a kinship
With these clear shadows.
They scatter, gather, scatter
All around my bare feet.

Two, who feel like two,
Sketch quick faces on my insteps.
Who are they? I don't want to know.
I want to see.

Why do these creatures come out to be
Family to me?
I am not in the water yet.
I wait a little.

Do they want to know me?
I have no more faces to give them
Than the moon has,
Scattering the eight fastidious feet of its light

Around the mountain behind my shoulder,
And now these small shoulders
And faces that seem
Not afraid of me.

Maybe they like to feel
Some warm voice
Singing out of my skin.
Why else would they touch me?

I don't know any language either.
But I hope
They can hear me, singing,
They owe me nothing.

But I believe them, I believe them:
These nearsighted gatherers of one another's flowers.
They touch my flinching instep, but now they float all the way across
The mauve mountain of the evening to rest on the little hill,
Your ankle. And now they are gone. And they do not laugh.

But you do,
My delight, whom I can see
In the dark.

OHIOAN PASTORAL

On the other side
Of Salt Creek, along the road, the barns topple
And snag among the orange rinds,
Oil cans, cold balloons of lovers.
One barn there
Sags, sags and oozes
Down one side of the copperous gulley.
The limp whip of a sumac dangles
Gently against the body of a lost
Bathtub, while high in the flint-cracks
And the wild grimed trees, on the hill,
A buried gas main
Long ago tore a black gutter into the mines.
And now it hisses among the green rings
On fingers in coffins.

THE FOX AT EYPE

He knows that all dogs bounding here and there, from the little vales all the way to the cliff-meadows and Thorncombe Beacon and beyond, are domestically forbidden to kill him. So every evening just before the end of twilight he emerges softly from the hedge across the lane and sits elegantly till darkness, gazing, with a certain weary amusement, into the middle distance of the sea.

FRESH WIND IN VENICE

North of one island
Where the tall tenements of old Jews freed by Napoleon
Loom and grieve stubbornly,

I found the fine gauze of willow that gathers.
It is the sea's fragrance that gathers
Me, heavily, more and more.

Out of this city, a slippery gathering
Of cities left empty, I went up there
North of one island,

And it is no use to try to gather
Anything new out of Venice, even the sea,
Even the dark eyes of the faces.

The only thing new in it is the light gathers
Gauze on willow
North of one island.

North of the city where factories
Murder the sun and what is left of the city
I found the sea gathering.

I found the sea gathering
All that was left.

BUTTERFLY FISH

Not five seconds ago, I saw him flutter so quick
And tremble with so mighty a trembling,
He was gone.
He left this clear depth of coral
Between his moments.
Now, he is here, back,
Slow and lazy.
He knows already he is so alive he can leave me alone,
Peering down, holding his empty mountains.
Happy in easy luxury, he grazes up his tall corals,
Slim as a stallion, serene on his far-off hillside,
His other world where I cannot see
His secret face.

ENTERING THE KINGDOM OF
THE MORAY EEL

There is no mystery in it so far
As I can see here.
Now the sun has gone down
Some little globules of mauve and beige still cling
Among coconuts and mangoes along the shore.
Over my right shoulder I glimpse a quick light.

I can believe in the moon stirring
Behind the hill at my back.
Before me, this small bay,
A beginning of the kingdom,
Opens its own half-moon.

Solitary,
Nearly naked, now,
I move in up to my knees.
Beneath the surface two shadows
Seem to move. But I know
They do not move.
They are only two small reefs of coral.

Some time this evening the moray eel will wake up
And swim from one reef to the other.
For now, this pathway of sand under water
Shines clear to me. I lift up my feet
And let the earth shift for itself.
Vicious, cold-blooded among his night branches,
The moray eel lets me
Shift for myself.
He is not going to visit his palaces
In my sight, he is not going to dance
Attention on the brief amazement of my life.
He is not going to surrender the spendid shadow
Of his throne. Not for my sake. Not even
To kill me.

AT PEACE WITH
THE OCEAN OFF MISQUAMICUT

A million rootlets
Shifting their dunes
Quiver a little on the deep
Clavicles of some body,
Down there, awhile.
It is still asleep, it is the Atlantic,
A stingray drowsing his fill of sunlight, a molting angel
Breathing the grateful water,
Praying face downward to a god I am afraid
To imagine.
What will I do when the stingray
And the angel
Wake?
Whose mercy am I going to throw
Myself upon?
When even the Atlantic Ocean
Is nothing more than
My brother the stingray.

IN MEMORY OF
MAYOR RICHARD DALEY

When you get down to it,
It, which is the edge of town,
You find a slab of gritstone
Face down in the burned stubble, the stinkweed,
The sumac, the elderberry.
Everything has gone out of the blossoms except the breath
Of rust from the railroad tracks.

And there in the river's graveyard
Nobody moves any more but you and me.
Ironweeds hunch up and live a long time, a strange forever.
They don't fall on the gravestones even in spring.
They don't fall in winter.
They go on living like the mystery
Of cancer.

One evening,
John Woods and somebody else and I
Killed the Chevvy motor down home
There, just above the singed-out brambles.
The citizens of the United States called that place
The Mill Field, that desolation, because
Some rum-bum back in the Depression flung
His last Bugler into the dead
Sawdust there.

We were there to sing drunk.
But a Model-T got
Between us and the B&O
And the Bareass Beach down the hill
And the river.

Halfway down the gouged bank
We found a flat gravestone

Nameless.
But we know the lost name.

When you get down to it,
It, on the edge of town,
You find this face.
It is a precious thing.
I took a good hard look at it
Before it was gone.
I can't get away from it.
This face fills me with grief as I sing to myself
In my sleep: Remember, remember
This is what you're up against.

LAMENT:
FISHING WITH RICHARD HUGO

If John Updike had been
Ed Bedford, his wife
Zetta would have called
Goose Prairie something high-toned.
Swan Meadow? The Ironic
Byronic Paradox in two
Eleatic heuristic footnotes?
Ed's dank tavern might have become
The Puce Nook, featuring
A menu illuminated by Doris Day,
With Updike composing the prose
Of Howard Johnson, accompanying himself
On an oboe, singing of tender
Succulent golden
French fries.

But now, though the hills around Goose Prairie
Are full of voices, nobody echoes
The rasping hinge of Zetta's quick cackle
Nor the slow sighs of Ed Bedford
Breaking the wind at dusk.
And I miss the unhorned
Elk that drifted across
The other side of Goose Prairie
Into pines that evening so long ago:
When Ed Bedford charged double for beer,
The pink flesh of trout from the Bumping River
Turned into you, and Howard's prose
Rendered into fish fat
And drifted, drifted
Over white water.

SHEEP IN THE RAIN

In Burgundy, beyond Auxerre
And all the way down the river to Avallon,
The grass lies thick with sheep
Shorn only a couple of days ago.
They shine all over their plump bodies
In the June mist.

Sheep eat everything
All the way down to the roots.
And maybe that is why
These explorers of the rain
Seem so relaxed in their browsing.
Someone has freed them only a little while
Into the fields, and they have a good life of it
While it lasts.

Burgundian farmers will return
Some morning soon,
And flock the fat sheep down a wall
Into glittering rocks.
Then a boy will go alone back into the grass
And care for the grass.
The farmers are kind to the grass.
They have to be.

A FLOWER PASSAGE

(in memory of Joe Shank, the diver)

Even if you were above the ground this year,
You would not know my face.
One of the small boys, one of the briefly green,
I prowled with the others along the Ohio,
Raised hell in the B&O boxcars after dark,
And sometimes in the evening
Chawed the knots out of my trousers
On the river bank, while the other
Children of blast furnace and mine
Fought and sang in the channel-current,
Daring the Ohio.

Shepherd of the dead, one of the tall men,
I did not know your face.
One summer dog day after another,
You rose and gathered your gear
And slogged downhill of the river ditch to dive
Into the blind channel. You dragged your hooks
All over the rubble sludge and lifted
The twelve-year bones.

Now you are dead and turned over
To the appropriate authorities, Christ
Have mercy on me, I would come to the funeral home
If I were home
In Martins Ferry, Ohio.
I would bring to your still face a dozen
Modest and gaudy carnations.

But I am not home in my place
Where I was born and my friends drowned.
So I dream of you, mourning.
I walk down the B&O track
Near the sewer main.
And there I gather, and here I gather

The flowers I only know best.
The spring leaves of the sumac
Stink only a little less worse
Than the sewer main, and up above that gouged hill
Where somebody half-crazy tossed a cigarette
Straight down into a pile of sawdust
In the heart of the LaBelle Lumber Company,
There, on the blank mill field, it is the blind and tough
Fireweeds I gather and bring home.
To you, for my drowned friends, I offer
The true sumac, and the foul trillium
Whose varicose bloom swells the soil with its bruise;
And a little later, I bring
The still totally unbelievable spring beauty
That for some hidden reason nobody raped
To death in Ohio.

YOUR NAME IN AREZZO

Five years ago I gouged it after dark
Against a little crippled olive's bark.
Somebody there, four, three, two years since then
Scattered the olives back to earth again.
Last summer in the afternoon I took
One tine, and hollowed out your name in rock,
A little one someone had left behind
The Duomo at the mercy of the wind.
The wind, as always sensitive to prayer,
Listed to mine, and left my pebble there,
Lifted your glistening name to some great height
And polished it to nothing overnight.
If the old olive wind will not receive
A name from me, even a name I love,
Fragile among Italian silences,
Your name, your pilgrim following cypresses,
I leave it to the sunlight, like the one
Landor the master left his voice upon.

DAWN NEAR AN OLD BATTLEFIELD, IN A TIME OF PEACE

Along the water the small invisible owls
Have fallen asleep in the poplars.
Standing alone here downshore on the river Yonne,
I can see only one young man pausing
Halfway over the stone bridge,
At peace with Auxerre.

How can he call to mind now
The thing he has never known:
One owl wing
Splayed in the morning wheat?
This young man
Sees only ripples on the Yonne.

How can he call to mind now,
And how can I,
His fathers, my fathers, crawling
Blind into the grain,
Scrambling among the scorched owls
And rats' wings for food?

All the young fathers
Are gone now. Mercy
On the young man
Who cannot call to mind now
The torn faces in the field.

Mercy on the pure Yonne washing his face in the water.

Mercy on me.

A FISHING SONG

I have never killed anybody
Except a gopher, and some fish.
I blatted fine gold hair all over hell's half acre
With a shotgun beside a road.
And one fish among many, a sunfish, I liked.
I cut his throat, and I ate him.
Whatever is left of the gopher's little ratface,
So far more sensitive than a song-thrush's face
When you see it up close,
Blows on a prairie somewhere.
Minnesota's dead animals are too many
For me to remember.
Yet I live with and caress the body
Of the sunfish. One out of many,
I caught him out of sheer accidental daring
As he tried to hide in the sunlight.
Leaping toward the Marsh Lake Dam,
He pretended he was merely a little splinter
In the general noon.
I knew better about his life.
Sweet plum, little shadow, he feeds my brother,
My own shadow.

ON HAVING MY POCKET PICKED
IN ROME

These hands are desperate for me to stay alive. They do not want to lose me to the crowd. They know the slightest nudge on the wrong bone will cause me to look around and cry aloud. Therefore the hands grow cool and touch me lightly, lightly and accurately as a gypsy moth laying her larvae down in that foregone place where the tree is naked. It is only when the hands are gone, I will step out of this crowd and walk down the street, dimly aware of the dark infant strangers I carry in my body. They spin their nests and live on me in their sleep.

A FINCH SITTING OUT
A WINDSTORM

Solemnly irritated by the turn
The cold air steals,
He puffs out his most fragile feathers,
His breast down,
And refuses to move.
If I were he,
I would not clamp my claws so stubbornly around
The skinny branch.
I would not keep my tiny glitter
Fixed over my beak, or return
The glare of the wind.
Too many Maytime snowfalls have taught me
The wisdom of hopelessness.

But the damned fool
Squats there as if he owned
The earth, bought and paid for.
Oh, I could advise him plenty
About his wings. Give up, drift,
Get out.

But his face is as battered
As Carmen Basilio's.
He never listens
To me.

CAPRICE

Whenever I get tired
Of human faces,
I look for trees.
I know there must be something
Wrong, either with me or Italy,
The south of the angels.
Nevertheless, I get away
Among good trees, there are
So many. The trouble is
They keep turning faces toward me
That I recognize:

Just north of Rome
An ilex and an olive tangled
Their roots together and stood one afternoon,
Caught in a ring of judas
And double cherry.
They glared at me, so bitter
With something they knew,
I shivered. They knew
What I knew:
One of those brilliant skeletons
Was going to shed her garlands
One of these days and turn back
Into a girl
Again.

Then we were all going to be
Sorry together.

A RAINBOW ON GARDA

The storm crawls down,
Dissolving the distances
Of the mountain as though
They were nothing.

The rain already
Hangs a gray shawl
In front of Bardolino.

The town is gone:

In the darkness of evening,
The darkness of high stone,
And a black swallow folding
Its face in one wing.

I too am ready
To fold my face.
I am used to night, the gray wall
Where swallows lie still.

But I am not ready for light
Where no light was,
Bardolino risen from the dead, blazing
A scarlet feather inside a wing.

Every fool in the world can see this thing,
And make no more
Of it than of Christ, frightened and dying
In the air, one wing broken, all alone.

MY NOTEBOOK

This friendly shadow of pine leaves
Goes by my side.
Its hands lie open to me on tables
When doors close.

Whenever I grow tired of speaking
And my dry lungs
Want only to hover still in my body,
It nods like rain.

The kindest moment it gave me came
One white afternoon:
The sun blanched all the walls in Grottaglie,
That southernmost olive.

Some nervous splinter
Worked under my skin.
I skinned my lips back to say something murderous,
Some savage thing.

It opened its pages
And showed me what it had:
Half of my name clear, the rest
Almost gone.

Streaked in a green stain,
An insect had flown in,
Quiet on the white leaf, paying
My name no mind.

LEAVE HIM ALONE

The trouble with me is
I worry too much about things that should be
Left alone.
The rain-washed stone beside the Adige where
The lizard used to lie in the sun
Will warm him again
In its own time, whether time itself
Be good or bad.
I sit on a hill
Far from Verona, knowing the vanity
Of trying to steal unaware on the lizards in the evening.
No matter how quickly
I pounce
Or slowly creep among the low evergreens
At the bend of the water,
He will be there
Or not there, just as
The sunlight pleases him.
The last feather of light fallen lazily down
Floats across the Adige and rests a long moment
On his lifted face.

REGRET FOR A SPIDER WEB

Laying the foundations of community, she labors all alone. Whether or not God made a creature as deliberately green as this spider, I am not the one to say. If not, then He tossed a star of green dust into one of my lashes. A moment ago, there was no spider there. I must have been thinking about something else, maybe the twenty-mile meadows along the slopes of the far-off mountain I was trying to name, or the huge snows clinging up there in summer, with their rivulets exploding into roots of ice when the night comes down. But now all the long distances are gone. Not quite three inches from my left eyelash, the air is forming itself into avenues, back alleys, boulevards, paths, gardens, fields, and one frail towpath shimmering as it leads away into the sky.

Where is she?

I can't find her.

Oh: resting beneath my thumbnail, pausing, wondering how long she can make use of me, how long I will have sense enough to hold still.

She will never know or care how sorry I am that my lungs are not huge magnificent frozen snows, and that my fingers are not firmly rooted in earth like the tall cypresses. But I have been holding my breath now for one minute and sixteen seconds. I wish I could tower beside her forever, and be one mountain she can depend upon. But my lungs have their own cities to build. I have to move, or die.

IN MEMORY OF
THE OTTOMANS

This man, mending his nets as the sun goes down, tells me religiously something I find dark: fog in the countryside of Otranto is unknown. As the starfish in the evening condense deep in the water, the light does not know what to do with itself. So the brown ridges down one side of the man's face turn green as spring rocks. Fog is unknown in Otranto, offshore from Otranto, behind Otranto. I can't believe he has never gone there. He won't say anything more about it, land or sea. What language do the hawks' tongues cry in for prayer, in that wilderness where the sea loses its way? I find this man dark. We both peer toward Greece, toward the horizon. The moon sways like a blunted scimitar.

TIME

Once, with a weak ankle, I tried to walk. All I could do was spin slowly a step or two, and then sit down. There has to be some balance of things that move on the earth. But this morning a small tern is flying full of his strength over the Ionian Sea. From where I stand, he seems to have only one wing. There is either something wrong with my eyes in the sunlight or something unknown to me about the shadow that hangs broken from his left shoulder. But the shadow is no good to me now. He has dropped it into the sea. There has to be some balance of things that move on the earth. But he is not moving on the earth. Both of my ankles are strong. My hair is gray.

TARANTO

Most of the walls
In what the Italians call
The old city
Are stained with suffering.

The dull yellow scars
Of whooping cough and catarrh
Hang trembling in the sea air, filaments
In an old man's lung.

American and German
Machine-gun bullets
Still pit the solitary hollows
Of shrines and arches.

To talk through is to become
Blood in a young man's lung,
Still living, still wondering
What in hell is going on.

But long before the city grew old, long
Before the Saracens fluttered like ospreys
Over the waters and sang
The ruin song,

Pythagoras walked here leisurely
Among the illegal generation
From Sparta, and Praxiteles
Left an astonished girl's face on a hillside

Where no hills were,
But the sea's.

A MOUSE TAKING A NAP

I look all alike to him, one blur of nervous mountains after another. I doubt if he loses any sleep in brooding and puzzling out why it is I don't like him. The huge slopes and valleys, golden as wild mustard flowers in midsummer, that he leaves lying open and naked down the sides of a Gorgonzola, seem to him only a discovery, one of the lonely paradises: nothing like the gray wound of a slag heap, nothing like the streams of copperous water that ooze out of the mine-mouths in southern Ohio. I wonder what it seems to him, his moment that he has now, alone with his own sunlight in this locked house, where all the cats are gone for a little while, hunting somebody else for a little while.

JEROME IN SOLITUDE

To see the lizard there,
I was amazed I did not have to beat
My breast with a stone.

If a lion lounged nearby,
He must have curled in a shadow of cypress,
For nobody shook a snarled mane and stretched out
To lie at my feet.

And, for a moment,
I did not see Christ retching in pain, longing
To clutch his cold abdomen,
Sagging, unable to rise or fall, the human
Flesh torn between air and air.

I was not even
Praying, unless: no,
I was not praying.

A rust branch fell suddenly
Down from a dead cypress
And blazed gold. I leaned close.
The deep place in the lizard's eye
Looked back into me.

Delicate green sheaths
Folded into one another.
The lizard was alive,
Happy to move.

But he did not move.
Neither did I.
I did not dare to.

AT THE END OF SIRMIONE

Conventional melancholy leaves me
Cold in this rain.
Across the lake water
The towns are not going to die.

They are folding, opening,
And folding in the mist.
Like a blind man, trusting
His garden, I can name them:

Bardolino thin on the longest shore.
Garda with two plateaus.
San Vigilio alone and half under water.
Maderno where travelers get drunk on lake water.

And Gargnano, Gargnano,
Where D. H. Lawrence and his donkey
Got lost on the mountain
On their way to church.

And Sirmione, here, the lizard of cisterns, turning
Silver as olive in the underside of rain
That leaves me alone on the cliff's grotto, anything
but cold.

VENICE

Crumbling into this world,
Into this world's sea, the green
Sea city decays.
The cats of the early evening,
Scrawny and sly,
Gloat among lengthening shadows of lions,
As the great Palladian wings lean toward the water and slowly
Fall and fall.
The city of shifting slime ought not to be
In this world.

It ought to drift only
In the mind of someone so desperately
Sick of this world,
That he dreams of himself walking
Under crystal trees,
Feeding the glass
Swans there, swans born
Not in the fragile calcium spun among feathers
But out of the horrifying fire that
A sullen laborer spins
In his frigid hands, just barely, just just barely not wringing
The swan's neck.

BETWEEN WARS

Flocks of green midges and the frail
Skeletons of mosquitoes hang
Hidden and calm beside some wall.
No matter why the swallows sang,
Last evening, and no matter now
Why they cavort, flutter, and soar.
They are not hungry anyhow.
There are no insects any more.

Far down the hill the Tuscan hawks
Fly wide awake. They surely see
Swallows scattering above blind rocks,
Daring the dreadful risk of joy.
A little while, the hawks will come
And shatter two or three or four,
The rest die where they started from.
There are no swallows any more:

Only a hundred fluttering by,
A million midges green and gone,
Two hawks amazing the blind sky,
And earth leaving itself alone.

AMONG SUNFLOWERS

You can stand in among them without
Being afraid.
Many of these faces
Look friendly enough,
Small ones will lean their damp golden foreheads
Against your body.
You can even lift your hands
And take some faces between them,
And draw them down
Near your own,
Gently.
Here,
And there,
A tall one, the stalk brittle and scarred,
Offers a haggard and defeated glance
With what would be good will in an old man,
And a shrug of forgiveness. There are old women
Among them who had no hope, dead,
Sprawled weightless in root-troughs.
So I can blame the faces for looking
Alike as they turn
Helplessly toward noon.
Any creature would be a fool to take the sun lightly,
The indifferent god of brief life, the
Small mercy.

IN A FIELD
NEAR METAPONTO

The huge columns, the temple of Apollo,
Have blown over in the nights.
I am tempted to say
It doesn't matter. The frightened men who crept forward
And cowered here, and turned back, are dead,
Of no account now.
But now
A great block of cloud falls over
In an instant, the sun
Lashes its flames on the sea's shivering spine
And glares straight down among the glittering hordes
Of poppies where I stand. They can do nothing.
They lean upward and lay
The secrets of their bodies bare to this light,
Till they die. I lean down,
Pluck one poppy, tuck it
Beside my ear like a Greek and stare for an instant
And then turn away.

CAMOMILA

Summer is not yet gone, but long ago the leaves have fallen. They never appeared to gather much sunlight or threw a measurable shade, even when they were most alive. They hid as long as they could beneath the white flowers and seemed to turn their faces away. They were like the faces of frightened people in a war. They silently wish they were anonymous, but they know that sooner or later someone will find them out. Everything secret to them will become commonplace to an army of invading strangers. Every stranger will know that each native of the defeated place was given at his birth, like a burden, the names of both his parents and his grandparents and great-grandparents, until there is scarcely enough room on a police form for all the names he carries around with him. Just like such brutally ransacked people, the camomila leaves turn their faces away. If I could look toward them long enough in this field, I think I would find them trying to hide their birthmarks and scars from me, pretending they had no beards or ribbons or long braids or half-legible letters from home hidden uselessly beneath their clothes. The faces of camomila leaves would wish me away again, wish me back into the sea again, wish me to leave them alone in peace.

YES, BUT

Even if it were true,
Even if I were dead and buried in Verona,
I believe I would come out and wash my face
In the chill spring.
I believe I would appear
Between noon and four, when nearly
Everybody else is asleep or making love,
And all the Germans turned down, the motorcycles
Muffled, chained, still.

Then the plump lizards along the Adige by San Giorgio
Come out and gaze,
Unpestered by temptation, across the water.
I would sit among them and join them in leaving
The golden mosquitoes alone.
Why should we sit by the Adige and destroy
Anything, even our enemies, even the prey
God caused to glitter for us
Defenseless in the sun?
We are not exhausted. We are not angry, or lonely,
Or sick at heart.
We are in love lightly, lightly. We know we are shining,
Though we cannot see one another.
The wind doesn't scatter us,
Because our very lungs have fallen and drifted
Away like leaves down the Adige,
Long ago.

We breathe light.

TO THE ADRIATIC WIND,
BECALMED

Come on.
Shift your wings a little.
You have plenty of strength left in your shoulders,
Your hawk mouth that does not care,
Your pure beak glittering like a scimitar
Proud of moonlight.
Come back to Venice.
Come back.
It's no skin off you.

The city is sagging.
One mere whir of one of your minor plumes
Could blow it down,
All the way into the water
Where the towers belong.
Already the golden horses of San Marco
Have stepped carefully down in the darkness,
Placed their frail ankles one after another
Over the damp cobbles, whickering lightly,
And gone. Come on.

There is no saving the horses now, they are lost
Inland somewhere, stumbling and shying
In the strange grass.
Now, in fresh dawn,
The opening morning glory of the sea,
Now is the time
To do beloved Venice a kindness.
Come, blow it the rest of the way.
Come on.

SNOWFALL:
A POEM ABOUT SPRING

The field mouse follows its own shadow
Up out of the twelve-inch fall
From a thin surface on one side of the path
Into a dark laurel some
Five feet away.

I take my little walk
Five feet beyond you and, all alone,
I follow the field mouse.
He and I track
The skeleton of an acorn, over
To the other side of the path.

He and I
Are gone a little,
But you
Somehow go over there at the other end of the snow tunnel, your
    throat

Bundled with laurel.

Ah, we breathe, we two,
We are not afraid of you, we will come out

And gather with you.

HONEY

My father died at the age of eighty. One of the last things he did in his life was to call his fifty-eight-year-old son-in-law "honey." One afternoon in the early 1930's, when I bloodied my head by pitching over a wall at the bottom of a hill and believed that the mere sight of my own blood was the tragic meaning of life, I heard my father offer to murder his future son-in-law. His son-in-law is my brother-in-law, whose name is Paul. These two grown men rose above me and knew that a human life is murder. They weren't fighting about Paul's love for my sister. They were fighting with each other because one strong man, a factory worker, was laid off from his work, and the other strong man, the driver of a coal truck, was laid off from his work. They were both determined to live their lives, and so they glared at each other and said they were going to live, come hell or high water. High water is not trite in southern Ohio. Nothing is trite along a river. My father died a good death. To die a good death means to live one's life. I don't say a good life.

I say a life.

WITH THE GIFT OF
A FRESH NEW NOTEBOOK I FOUND
IN FLORENCE

On the other side of the bridge,
Over the Arno,
Across the Ponte Vecchio, across
The street from the Pitti Palace, below the garden,
Under the shadow of the fortress,
I found this book,
This secret field of the city down over the hill
From Fiesole.

Nobody yet has walked across and sat down
At the edge under a pear tree
To savor the air of the natural blossoms and leave them
Alone, and leave the heavy place alone.

The pages have a light spirit
That will rise into blossom and harvest only
After your hand touches them.
Then the book will grow
Lighter and lighter as the seasons pass.
But, so far, this field is only
A secret of snow.

Now this slender field lies only a little uphill
From the river, and the pale water
Seems to be turning everything
It mirrors into snow.
It is that snow before anyone
Has walked across it
Slowly as children walk on their way to school
In the glittering Ohio morning,
Or quickly as the breathless
Ermine scamper upward through the light crust
In one indeterminate spot and then stitch

A threadwork across the whiteness and suddenly
Vanish as though blown like flakes back upward.

Red and white flowers lie quietly all around
The edges of the field,
And it doesn't matter that they don't grow there now.
For one time they grew there
Long enough to make the air
Vivid when they vanished.

I suppose I could imagine
The trees that haven't yet grown here.
But I would rather leave them to find their way
Alone, like seedlings lost in a cloud of snowflakes.
I would rather leave them alone, even
In my imagination, or, better still,
Leave them to you.

LEAVING THE TEMPLE IN NÎMES

And, sure enough,
I came face to face with the spring.
Down in the wet darkness of the winter moss
Still gathering in the Temple of Diana,
I came to the trunk of a huge umbrella pine
Vivid and ancient as always,
Among the shaped stones.
I couldn't see the top of the branches,
I stood down there in the pathway so deep.
But a vine held its living leaves all the way down
To my hands. So I carry away with me
Four ivy leaves:

In gratitude to the tall pale girl
Who still walks somewhere behind the pine tree,
Slender as her hounds.
In honor of the solitary poet,
Ausonius, adorer of the southern hillsides
Who drank of the sacred spring
Before he entered this very holy place
And slowly tuned the passionate silver
Of his Latin along the waters.

And I will send one ivy leaf, green in winter,
Home to an American girl I know.
I caught a glimpse of her once in a dream,
Shaking out her dark and adventurous hair.
She revealed only a little of her face
Through the armfull of pussy willow she gathered
Alive in spring,
Alive along the Schuylkill in Philadelphia.

She will carry this ivy leaf from Diana's pine
As she looks toward Camden, across the river,
Where Walt Whitman, the chaste wanderer

Among the live-oaks, the rain, railyards and battlefields,
Lifts up his lovely face
To the moon and allows it to become
A friendly ruin.
The innocent huntress will come down after dark,
Brush the train smoke aside, and leave alone together
The old man rooted in an ugly place
Pure with his lovingkindness,
And a girl with an ivy leaf revealing her face
Among fallen pussy willow.

A WINTER DAYBREAK ABOVE VENCE

The night's drifts
Pile up below me and behind my back,
Slide down the hill, rise again, and build
Eerie little dunes on the roof of the house.
In the valley below me,
Miles between me and the town of St.-Jeannet,
The road lamps glow.
They are so cold, they might as well be dark.
Trucks and cars
Cough and drone down there between the golden
Coffins of greenhouses, the startled squawk
Of a rooster claws heavily across
A grove, and drowns.
The gumming snarl of some grouchy dog sounds,
And a man bitterly shifts his broken gears.
True night still hands on,
Mist cluttered with a racket of its own.

Now on the mountainside,
A little way downhill among turning rocks,
A square takes form in the side of a dim wall.
I hear a bucket rattle or something, tinny,
No other stirring behind the dim face
Of the goatherd's house. I imagine
His goats are still sleeping, dreaming
Of the fresh roses
Beyond the walls of the greenhouse below them
And of lettuce leaves opening in Tunisia.

I turn, and somehow
Impossibly hovering in the air over everything,
The Mediterranean, nearer to the moon
Than this mountain is,
Shines. A voice clearly
Tells me to snap out of it. Galway

Mutters out of the house and up the stone stairs
To start the motor. The moon and the stars
Suddenly flicker out, and the whole mountain
Appears, pale as a shell.

Look, the sea has not fallen and broken
Our heads. How can I feel so warm
Here in the dead center of January? I can
Scarcely believe it, and yet I have to, this is
The only life I have. I get up from the stone.
My body mumbles something unseemly
And follows me. Now we are all sitting here strangely
On top of the sunlight.

A NOTE ON THE TEXT
OF THIS JOURNEY

On March 17, 1980, a Xerox copy of the manuscript of *This Journey* was given to Galway Kinnell when he went to see James at Mount Sinai Hospital in New York. James wrote the following note to Galway: "I think the book is more or less done." He also wrote down the dedication for Galway and the title *This Journey,* which he had written in a note to Frank MacShane earlier in March. Another Xerox copy was given to Donald Hall when he came to visit James at Calvary Hospital in the Bronx. Later in the spring, copies were also sent to Robert Bly, Hayden Carruth, John Logan and Robert Mezey, close friends and fellow poets. It had been James's custom to give them copies of his manuscripts for their suggestions and comments.

In August of 1980 Donald Hall and his wife Jane Kenyon met me at the home of Galway and Inés Kinnell in Vermont to discuss the manuscript, and the comments of all the poets, who had written and telephoned their ideas, were talked over. It was decided to remove two unfinished poems and three others, and a few changes in the order of the poems were made. The manuscript was then typed by our sister-in-law, Helen Wright, and *This Journey* was complete.

—ANNE WRIGHT

ABOUT THE AUTHOR

JAMES WRIGHT was born in Martins Ferry, Ohio, on December 13, 1927. After graduating from Kenyon College he was a Fulbright Scholar at the University of Vienna before completing his doctorate at the University of Washington. His first book, *The Green Wall,* won the Yale Series of Younger Poets award in 1954. His other books include *Saint Judas, The Branch Will Not Break, Shall We Gather at the River, Collected Poems* (which won the Pulitzer Prize in 1972), *Moments of the Italian Summer, Two Citizens,* and *To a Blossoming Pear Tree.* He died in 1980.